THE

CHURCH UNDER END-TIME ATTACK!

Prophetic Parallels From 9-11

DR. JOE VAN KOEVERING

Unless otherwise indicated, all scripture quotations are taken from the King James Version of the Bible.

**THE CHURCH UNDER
END-TIME ATTACK!**

THE CHURCH UNDER END-TIME ATTACK

TABLE OF CONTENTS

OUR RESPONSE

THE CHURCH UNDER END-TIME ATTACK

INTRODUCTION

This is a prophetic word for the Church; for the Church is under end-time attack. God began to give me and show me prophetic and spiritual parallels from the September 11th attack on America.

Just as America was attacked on September 11, 2001, the end-time Church is also under attack. The physical attack upon the head and the heart of this nation parallels the spiritual attack upon the head and the heart of the Church. The same exact spirit which instigated and which initiated this act of lawless terror upon unsuspecting people in America is a prophetic picture to the saints of God as to the same exact spirit which wars against the souls of unsuspecting and unaware saints in this very hour.

A final hour and last day war has now begun between the plans of God and the plans of Satan for this earth.

The Lord spoke to me and said, "Son, I want you to observe the significant elements of this attack on America. I want you to see and I want you to learn the parallels to the significant elements of how the spirit behind this terrorist act seeks to bring terror into the Church of Jesus Christ."

If that is true, then we must have a foundational starting point. What and who is the true and real spirit that fostered, and gave birth, and who is behind this act of terror?

"Little children, it is the last time: and as ye have heard that antichrist shall come, even now are there many antichrists; whereby we know that it is the last time. They went out from us, but they were not of us; for if they had been of us, they would no doubt have continued with us: but they went out, that they might be made manifest that they were not all of us.

"But ye have an unction from the Holy One, and ye know all things. I have not written unto you because ye know not the truth, but because ye know it, and that no lie is of the truth. Who is a liar but he that denieth that Jesus is the Christ? He is antichrist, that denieth the Father and the Son. Whosoever denieth the Son, the same hath not the Father: (but) he that acknowledgeth the Son hath the Father also."

—I John 2:18-23

Who is Antichrist? He that denies Jesus is the Christ: he is Antichrist. You can say out of your mouth you've got God with you all day long, but if you deny that the Father and the Son are One, you have not the Father. That's what He said. "Whosoever denieth the Son, the same hath not the Father: but he that acknowledgeth the Son hath the Father also."

"Beloved, believe not every spirit, but try the spirits whether they are of God: because many false prophets are gone out into the world. Hereby know ye the Spirit of God: Every spirit that confesseth that Jesus Christ is come in the flesh is of God: And every spirit that confesseth not that Jesus Christ is come in the flesh is not of God: and this is that spirit of antichrist, whereof ye have heard that it should come; and even now already is it in the world.

"Ye are of God, little children, and have overcome them: because greater is he that is in you, than he that is in the world."

—I John 4:1-4

There's going to be a lot of holy, religious sounding spirits that aren't of God. You've got to test them. Here is the test and make a big note of this: "Every spirit that confesses that Jesus Christ is come in the flesh **IS** of God: And every spirit that confesses not that Jesus Christ is come in the flesh **IS NOT** of God."

There's no debate about it. We don't need to be politically correct about this. He makes it very clear that if you deny that He came in the flesh, if you are motivated by a spirit that denies that Jesus came in the flesh as Christ, you are not being controlled by a spirit that comes from God.

And He calls it clearly what it is.

He said, "This is that spirit of **Antichrist**, whereof ye have heard that it should come; and even now already is it in the world."

Thank God for verse 4: "Ye are of God, little children, and have overcome them: because greater is He that is in you, than he that is in the world."

Let's examine the term "Antichrist." This term "Antichrist" is a word found only in the Epistles of John. It can mean "against Christ." It can also mean "instead of Christ." In fact, W.E. Vines' **The Great Expository Dictionary of New Testament Words** combines those two meanings with the word "Antichrist."

He writes the meaning, "One, who assuming the guise of Christ, actually opposes Christ." So we believe that the spirit of Antichrist will try to be Christ but will clearly oppose Christ. "Someone who will be imitating Christ and who will be against Christ and what He stands for."

The Apostle John informs us that many Antichrists have already entered into the world. From the time of the birth of the Messiah to the Early Church, there were many false prophets and many false Christs. This was a sign that Jesus gave to us. If we catalog history, we can find that to be the case.

On four different occasions, John uses this unique word "Antichrist," or "**ANTOS CHRISTOS**," and it is to define those who are in opposition of the "Son-ship" of Christ.

SPIRIT OF ANTICHRIST

There is a spirit of Antichrist that was in the world then, and has continued to exist in the world up until now.

These verses, along with Old Testament prophets, taught, as well as Jesus Himself affirmed, the two key elements that are involved here. There is an Antichrist spirit and there is also a physical personage, who will be a man, who will fully yield himself to that spirit. He will become known as *the* Antichrist.

He isn't going to look like Antichrist when he first comes. He's going to look like Christ, supposedly, to those that follow him when he first comes. But he will literally oppose all that stands for Christ and for God. Remember, there are two elements.

John defines the spirit of Antichrist and states that he will deny three specific things. What are they?

"Who is a liar but he that denieth that Jesus is the Christ? He is antichrist, that denieth the Father and the Son."
—I John 2:22

It says in this portion of scripture that the spirit of Antichrist will:

1. Deny the deity of Jesus.
2. Deny that Jesus Christ is the Son of God.
3. Deny the relationship between the Father and the Son.

In these writings, John distinguished the spirit of the Antichrist from the ultimate personage of the Antichrist. Since John taught that there are many Antichrists, some incorrect prophecy teaching and incorrect eschatological preachers have somehow referred and concluded that this Antichrist was only a spirit and would not eventually be an individual. That is not true. It is true, however, that there is a spirit of Antichrist that's been on the earth since John wrote the Epistles.

It's very easy to prove if you look in the Greek language, because if you look at a Greek interlinear Bible, that same scripture passage states, "Who is the liar if it is not the one that denies that Jesus is the Christ. This is the Antichrist." Now the Greek text translated "the Antichrist" is "**HO ANTICHRISTOS.**" "**Ho**" is a definite article meaning "the"; and John refers to "an" Antichrist; not just "an" Antichrist, but he refers to him as "the" antichrist. "**HO ANTICHRISTOS**" means ___**THE**___ Antichrist. So he is referring to an upcoming eventual specific person.

Many referred to the Antichrist: Jesus, Paul, Daniel and others. Many different names and titles are given to this personage: "the Assyrian," "the little horn," "the beast," "the man of son," etc. There will be a person that emerges in the end time scene who will become the Antichrist, because he will fully yield himself to this spirit that now roams the earth and exists in the earth.

Before the person known as the Antichrist emerges on the scene, we will first see and experience the *spirit behind* the Antichrist. Before the man wages war on the world, the spirit will wage war on the Church.

Even though it isn't politically correct, I'm going to show you what it is.

The major rift between Islam and Christianity is the belief that Jesus was, Jesus is now, and Jesus will forever be the Son of the living God. According to the Quran, the Islam Holy Book, Islam says good and nice things about our Jesus.

They will even go so far as to say that Jesus was born of the Virgin Mary, referring to the Virgin Mary by name. The Quran teaches that Jesus was not, and never will be, the Son of God. The Quran teaches that Jesus was simply a prophet; and there were other prophets that followed Him.

I've got news for my Muslim friends. First John tells me that there's going to be many false prophets. Yes, Mohammed is a false prophet. I don't mean disrespect on anyone's faith. I don't mean disrespect on anyone's religion or what they've come to conclude. I challenge you, if you teach the Quran, and you believe the Quran, and you believe the words of Mohammed, I challenge you to go check out what Mohammed said and compare it to the Holy Scriptures. One cannot believe both.

True Christianity believes that Jesus is the Son of the living God, and if that fact is not true, then our entire faith crumbles.

The basic tenet of Islam declares that God has no Son, in direct opposition to the declaration of John. We've just read that the spirit of the person who denies the relationship of Jesus and the Father is the spirit of Antichrist.

Again, this is not politically correct, but I must speak the truth. *The spirit behind radical Islam is the spirit of Antichrist!* Furthermore, should a Muslim come to power in the next few months or a few years, and he gets the entire

Muslim world united behind him in an effort to combat Christianity, including a concentrated effort to combat the nation of Israel, I'm here to tell you that person is **the Antichrist**.

As Christians living in this monumental prophetic moment of history, we find ourselves, just as America now finds herself, going to war against this end time spirit.

"Thou therefore endure hardness, as a good soldier of Jesus Christ."
—*II Timothy 2:3*

Before September 11th I preached a message entitled, "What Does This Look Like, A Holiday Inn?" From the New Testament, I proved that we are all called to be soldiers in an army. I preached that, as Christians, we cannot go A.W.O.L. We've got a battle and a fight on our hands. And look what happened a few months later? We're at war.

I'm not talking about the war in the United States or in the Middle East. I'm talking about the war in the house of God. I'm talking about the war that the Church is called to right now. You and I are in war; we are at battle with an end time spirit known as the spirit of Antichrist. We need to wake up!

"Be sober, be vigilant; because your adversary the devil, as a roaring lion, walketh about, seeking whom he may devour: Whom resist stedfast in the faith, knowing that the same afflictions are accomplished in your brethren that are in the world."
—*I Peter 5:8-9*

"...be strong in the Lord, and in the power of his might. Put on the whole armour of God, that ye may be able to stand against the wiles of the devil. For we wrestle not against flesh and blood, but against principalities, against powers, against the rulers of the darkness of this world, against spiritual wickedness in high places. Wherefore take unto you the whole armour of God, that ye may be able to withstand in the evil day, and having done all, to stand."
— *Ephesians 6:10-13*

Paul knew that there was coming an ***evil day***. If we're not living in an evil day right now, I don't know what it is. It can't be the tribulation period yet, for that is an evil day reserved for the very end.

However, we are in the midst of the greatest spiritual struggle that the Church has ever known. Our time is almost gone. It's either now or never, for this evil day is upon us now.

The spirit that wants to ultimately consume a man to have authority in this earth to perpetrate the greatest horrendous act upon Christianity and Judaism is now loose in this earth. This spirit has declared war against the Church. **Christian, you are under attack!**

What are you going to do about this new era that we have entered into here in America?

Your enemy has devices. Your enemy has strategies that he's going to use against you. We must not remain ignorant of them. We've got to resist the enemy!

We must learn how to put on the whole armor of God and withstand this spirit. We are now in the midst of the evil day, and just as our beloved nation has entered into a new day, so too the saints of God, the true Church of Jesus Christ, has entered this new and final day of the end time struggle against the original terrorist spirit. The original terrorist spirit is the spirit of Antichrist.

God showed me seven keys, or seven parallels, between the September 11th attack on our nation and the spiritual attack upon the saints.

When God gave me these seven, He also then showed me seven more parallels on how our nation responded. There are seven parallels of how the natural attack came on our nation linked to the spiritual attack upon the saints. I want you to be armed for your struggle. You're under attack. Let this be warning in advance of what's coming to your house and my house, and your life and my life, because they parallel what we've seen.

THE CHURCH UNDER END-TIME ATTACK

PARALLEL

THE ENEMY IS SUBVERSIVE

This is the first word the Lord spoke to me. This enemy that struck America was subversive. You've got to understand something. Your enemy is subtle. Your enemy is strategic. Your enemy is hiding, waiting for YOU!

These terrorists blended right into our present society. I'm sure you've seen the television interviews that said, "Oh man, they lived right over there...I don't know; I'm totally shocked...I mean they were quiet...They'd come in at strange hours of the night...Oh man, we didn't have a clue; didn't even understand...."

They had in their possession a handbook on terrorism, a manual from Osama bin Laden's school of terror. They were instructed, "Don't have any facial hair. Act normal..." There were pages and pages of instruction on how not to draw attention to themselves.

They were subversive until the moment when they wanted to attack.

You must understand this about the enemy of your soul. The enemy of your soul will do everything he can to blend into your life somewhere. The enemy of your soul wants to hide subtly, quietly, subversively — blend in and hide in some unnoticed place of your daily routine and your daily habits until the chosen moment to strike.

Many Christians live with an enemy spirit; and they don't even realize it! They don't even realize that spirit is ultimately going to try to kill them at an appointed time. Every day they get up and they stroke it, they talk to it, they take it with them to work, they take it with them to the bank; some of them bring it to church. That "thing" is a SPIRIT that is lying in wait, dormant, subversively, cunningly, subtly. You see, that thing that wants to kill you, it doesn't look like much right now. It just looks small and insignificant. You could deal with it at any time if you really knew.

If we would have really known where those terrorists were, we could have dealt with it and the attack never would have happened. We didn't even observe the terrorists in training right here in our own country. We didn't even know it. They just blended right in and looked like some of us well-meaning Americans.

That's the way the devil is with saints. They have "things" with them that just subtly stay there in some recess of their life, some part of their daily routine. Maybe you're so used to seeing it, you don't even know that it wants to kill you. It's so blended in and so subtle that it's become normal for you to think that certain way, talk that certain way, act that certain way, or yield that certain way. This has become **normal** to you.

I've got news for you, though. God has not called you to be "normal." What are you trying to be normal for, anyhow?

"Well, you know they make fun of me when I pray all the time and I bring my Bible to work." Let them laugh at you. Let them make fun of you. Don't you try to blend in and be normal. God's called you to be peculiar!

"But ye are a chosen generation, a royal priesthood, an holy nation, a peculiar people; that ye should show forth the praises of him who hath called you out of darkness into his marvellous light."
—I Peter 2:9

It says, "You are a chosen generation." Do you believe we are part of a chosen generation? This generation right now is a chosen generation. You are a royal priesthood. You are a holy nation. You're a peculiar people. Why?

So YOU can "show forth the praises of Him who's called you out of darkness and into His marvelous light." You're not merely natural. You're called to be supernatural. You've got a natural, and I've got a natural, too. But God wants to put His **super** on my **natural**. You're called to be supernatural, not just natural anymore. So don't let something just blend in.

Please observe the attack on America and learn from it. Your enemy, too, will be subtle and subversive. Don't let him hide somewhere in your life!

THE CHURCH UNDER END-TIME ATTACK

PARALLEL

THE ENEMY PATIENTLY WAITED UNTIL THE RIGHT TIME TO STRIKE

According to our official reports, this attack was years in the making. When I heard that, I said, "That's just like the way the devil works." That's the way that spirit that we war against works. He isn't going to come urgently knocking on your life tomorrow. He's going to wait for a particular moment, a little incident here, take another little step over here, a small move over there, and patiently wait for the right moment to strike.

The terrorist leadership had to plan it. Then they had to recruit the needed men. Then they had to train them. They had to build this team of many terrorists. There are still more on the loose! They are trying to find them right now. Then after they recruited and trained them for all these years, when everything was just right, they seized the moment and they struck.

We've been told that only 21 days earlier than September 11th, the CIA was informed to find two of the perpetrators. According to **NEWSWEEK** magazine, "Al Matta and Al Hazik Hazmi would resonate with intelligence officials on September 11th. Both men were listed among the hijackers of American Airlines flight 77, the airline that dive-bombed the Pentagon. Indeed, when one intelligence official saw the names of the listed suspects, he uttered an expletive. Why? Because just three weeks earlier, on August 21, the CIA asked the INS to keep a watch out for Al Matta. The INS reported that the man was already in the country. His only declared address was some Marriott Hotel in New York. The CIA sent the FBI to find Al Matta and his associates. The gumshoes were still looking on September 11th."

See, any delay in locating and eliminating your enemy may be costly. It will be deadly. Any delay in finding and locating the enemy of your soul before he seizes the moment against you could be deadly.

The enemy doesn't strike when he knows he will be found. He doesn't strike at you when you're strong and he knows that he will lose. These guys waited for the right, opportune time. They could have walked in there a week earlier or a week later, and maybe somebody would have noticed something, somebody would have spotted them. But they waited. They waited for the right time. Your enemy waits until your vulnerable moment and then he rises up.

It's normally not on Sundays that he tempts you. As Christians, you're strong; you're prayed up. You've been to church, worshipping God.

But Monday morning might be different. Friday morning might be different. The enemy doesn't wait until you're on the mountaintop. He doesn't attack you when everything is going right, and when you are spiritually strong. He waits to find a vulnerable moment. He doesn't strike when you are spiritually strong. No, he waits for the right time to strike. We all have and experience those "down" times. We all have weak and vulnerable moments.

"Does that mean there's no hope?"

No. What then are we to do, knowing that one has weak moments? Simple, do not fight alone! Find somebody who will stand by your side and fight with you, because when you're down, they'll be strong. When you're vulnerable, they'll be praising God. Find somebody to link arms with you spiritually, because your enemy is waiting for a weak moment in your life. He will find one sometime. He'll look until he finds a weak moment.

I need somebody in my life. I need a group of people in my life that will pray for me when I don't feel like praying.

That's why you need a strong church. You need a place where you go to meet God, hear from God, worship God and serve God. You can't be out there in today's world roaming around like a Lone Ranger, trying to make it in this hour.

The spirit of Antichrist is loose in the earth and you're going to get eaten up and sucked down. Don't fight alone. You need fellow saints; you need the brethren. You need someone at your side standing with you, ready to help fight off that attack and that temptation on your behalf when you find yourself at your weakest moment.

"Not forsaking the assembling of ourselves together, as the manner of some is; but exhorting one another: and so much the more, as ye see the day approaching."

— Hebrews 10:25

Do you see the day approaching?

I'm telling you, it's coming now. Everybody sees it approaching now. What does that scripture say to you? "Just stay out there and let the winds of temptation knock you down?" No! "Run to the assembling together of your fellow saints, and exhort and strengthen one another."

Don't try to stand alone in this hour. Church, observe and learn. Your enemy is waiting to strike, so beware.

THE CHURCH UNDER END-TIME ATTACK

PARALLEL

THE NOTICEABLE AND VISIBLE SITE OF OUR STRENGTH WAS THE TARGET

A journalist for **TIME** magazine reported on the September 11th attack and observed, "If you want to humble an empire, it will make sense to maim its cathedrals. They are symbols of its faith. And when they crumbled and burned it tells us that we are not so powerful, and we can't be safe. The Twin Towers of the World Trade Center planted at the base of Manhattan Island, with the Statue of Liberty as their sentry and the Pentagon a squat concrete fort on the banks of the Potomac, are the *sanctuaries of money and power* that our enemies may imagine define us.

"But that assumes our faith rests on what we can buy and build, and that has never been America's true God." These are rather profound words from a secular journalist, calling the Twin Towers our "sanctuary of money." Did the World Trade Center represent the false idols of our nation?

The World Trade Center was the symbol of America's economic power, and this was the target.

As with America, so it is with every person, and therefore every Christian. ***Your greatest strength is also potentially your greatest weakness.*** Show me the area of your life where God has gifted you, graced you and given you a talent, and ability, anointing and authority, and I will show you the area which in your life you will fight your greatest battle. Your enemy will fight the hardest to bring you down and bring you to ruins. You show me someone who has a mantle of financial increase on their life, and I'll show you someone who has gone through cycles of financial calamity, maybe bankruptcy.

Why? Because there's a mantle on their life to put finances into the Gospel.

What is the greatest threat to the enemy is what the enemy attacks the most. You show me someone like a mother or someone whose greatest calling on their life is their children, because God knows that they're going to raise up mighty warriors for the Kingdom of God, and I'll show you the area where that woman will fight her greatest battles. Their heart is where their calling is. Your children are your calling, your anointing, and your areas of assignment.

You may be called to equip your children to do something great. But you will also fight your greatest battle in that same arena.

So, show me the arena where you fight your biggest battles, and I'll predict where your greatest victory will come. You show me the area of your greatest strength, and it is potentially your greatest weakness. Where you're a threat to the forces of hell is the very place where you will wage your greatest battles. We must understand this.

America is prosperous for one reason: In order to fund and finance the preaching of the Gospel. God's prosperity has come upon this land because we've stood with Israel and we have financed the missions to the world. We don't have huge oil fields like the Arabs do, funding their agendas. The prosperity that this nation has is because God has given grace to this nation.

The minute this nation neglects, forgets and fails to remember why God gave us that prosperity, He could take it away in a moment.

Why? It's this little thing called pride. You show me someone who has an anointing in a certain area, a gifting, and a talent and a strength in a certain area; they're good at it and they know it; they're good at it and it's easy, it just comes easy to them — do you know what? The devil will be right there to try to elevate pride in that area.

You can sing well and you can move people with your voice, but you will eventually have to fight pride in that area. Whatever it is you're good at, whatever your strength is, there's pride just right beneath the surface. If the devil can ever wipe away the security and get that pride out, what was your greatest strength is potentially your biggest weakness.

"Pride goeth before destruction, and an haughty spirit before a fall."

—Proverbs 16:18

"...God resisteth the proud, and giveth grace to the humble."

—I Peter 5:5

The only thing that can stop you is pride.

This attack will come at the symbol of our greatest strength in an attempt to uncover any pride that may be just beneath the surface of our lives, and therefore potentially become your greatest weakness.

"Wherefore let him that thinketh he standeth take heed lest he fall."

—I Corinthians 10:12

Do you hear the warning in that? The area where you stand the tallest, take heed lest you fall. On September 11th, we saw our tallest symbol of our greatest strength fall before our eyes. This is a parallel to us. The Bible is literally filled with examples of this. Men like Sampson who fought his greatest battles in the arena of God's greatest anointing. What about David? David's greatest strength and anointing was as a warrior, yet because he had blood on his hands, it kept him from the greatest thing that God wanted for him to do.

Peter is a perfect example of this, also. Do you remember, Jesus turned to Peter and said, "You're going to deny me." Now, a wise man would have fallen at the feet of Jesus and said, "Oh, Jesus, help me. I don't want to do that. Oh, Jesus, please, you know I recognize you as a prophet and obviously you spoke that to me, and I don't want to do that. I need your strength to help me from doing that."

Yet, he didn't respond in that humble manner. He immediately got proud: "I'll never do that." Jesus turned to him and said, "Get thee behind me, Satan." Suddenly, his greatest strength was the place where the devil got a foothold and access into his mind and in his thinking. And Jesus had to rebuke him.

That same courageous Peter that was ready to take on a battalion for Jesus a few hours later was running from a little girl that said, "Oh, you're one of those disciples with Jesus." The same guy that was ready to attack a battalion was running from a little girl. What happened?

The grace lifted and the hedge came down. You are able to stand against temptation, not because you're so spiritual. You are able to stand against temptation because you're relying on the grace of God.

The devil will come at the point of your greatest strength, because he knows that it potentially can be your greatest weakness because of pride. Church, we must learn this important truth in order to stand against the attack of Satan.

THE CHURCH UNDER END-TIME ATTACK

PARALLEL

THE STRIKE CAME AT THE TOP OF THE WORLD TRADE CENTER

Back in 1993 these same enemy forces had bombed the World Trade Center at the bottom. The attack didn't succeed. But this time, they struck the top or at "the head."

I see a twofold meaning in interpretation and application of this. First of all we can apply it individually. Your enemy will always strike at your **head** to deceive you and to destroy you.

"For though we walk in the flesh, we do not war after the flesh:(For the weapons of our warfare are not carnal, but mighty through God to the pulling down of strong holds;) Casting down imaginations, and every high thing that exalteth itself against the knowledge of God, and bringing into captivity every thought to the obedience of Christ."
—II Corinthians 10:3-5

Those strongholds are in your mind. You see, your warfare will always involve your head. Your greatest thoughts. Your battleground in the fight is always fought in the arena of the mind. If you as a Christian do not learn how to control the thoughts that come to your mind, you will never walk in victory. You will falter if you just let your thoughts and your mind just run where it wants to go. If you don't ever wrestle and fight with those strongholds in your imagination, and deal with those thoughts and bring them captive, the devil will get you doing whatever he wants you to do.

The enemy of your soul won't attack your spirit directly. He'll come at your mind.

I submit this to you. Even if he does come after you in the natural, which he does in your body, the second after he does something to strike your body, he strikes your mind.

"Well you know, Aunt Minnie had cancer, that's probably what that is." You get some little pain in the morning, the devil will jab you with one of his darts in your physical man.

"Well, you know Dad, you know he had that terrible heart condition? And he started out with those same type of pains you are having now."

No!

Do you see what the devil is doing? He's attacking your head. He's attacking the top. Individually you've got to understand to renew your mind. That's why we need to renew our minds to the Word of God. We need to start thinking the thoughts of God. You've got to change your thoughts, including how you think of yourself.

Individually, the devil strikes your head, but corporately, the enemy will also strike at our head.

The enemy always tries to attack the leadership in the church. Satan knows that if he can take out the ones up at the top, then the whole house can come tumbling down. This is why you must pray for our leaders.

"I exhort therefore, that, first of all, supplications, prayers, intercessions, and giving of thanks, be made for all men; For kings, and for all that are in authority; that we may lead a quiet and peaceable life in all godliness and honesty."
—I Timothy 2:1-2

That authority is two-fold. Not only is that civil authority, but it's also spiritual authority. We're so easy to be critical of our leaders. You've never walked one day in that person's shoes. You've never had to face what they face.

Your new level of spirituality will come with a new area of spiritual disciplines that's going to be required of you. When you move up, you're now a greater threat to the enemy. You're putting yourself out on the front lines. You're out at that point of attack. Our pastors, our shepherds and our spiritual leaders are right out there at the point of attack for us, paving our way. Pray for your leaders. You need to cover your pastor and your spiritual leaders in prayer every single day. Why? Because the enemy is specifically attacking the head.

"Obey them that have the rule over you, and submit yourselves: for they watch for your souls, as they that must

give account, that they may do it with joy, and not with grief: for that is unprofitable for you.

"Pray for us: for we trust we have a good conscience, in all things willing to live honestly."

—Hebrews 13:17-18

God is saying when you remember, and you obey and you submit, you must pray for your spiritual leaders.

So observe and learn. The strike came at the top.

THE CHURCH UNDER END-TIME ATTACK

PARALLEL

OUR NATION'S ASSETS WERE USED AGAINST US

The enemy took our planes, filled with our people, filled with our fuel, and used them to attack us. They hid within our own cities. They even received flight training within our own aviation schools. They sat right there in our "own house" and let us teach them how to kill us.

The enemy of your soul will always try to steal your power and steal your authority; and then use it against you. This is how he works. The devil hasn't got some secret spiritual weapon in hell that he's going to spring out on you. No, he's going to use your very own authority against you. He's going to use your own words against you. He's going to use your own seeds against you. He's going to take your authority away from you through ignorance and through deception. That's the greatest weapon he's got.

The devil has no tools other than deception. He can tempt and he can accuse, but the greatest thing he has is deception.

In fact, the word for "devil" in the New Testament literally means "deceiver"… Yes, he's an accuser… And yes, he's a tempter. But his greatest tool is deception. What does that mean? That means he's got to get you to believe a lie. He's got to get you thinking a lie, talking a lie, and living something that isn't true in order to take life from you, rob from you, and to try to kill you.

"In meekness instructing those that oppose themselves; if God peradventure will give them repentance to the acknowledging of the truth; And that they may recover themselves out of the snare of the devil, who are taken captive by him at his will."
—II Timothy 2:25-26

There are multitudes of Christians who, through deception, have literally handed over their authority and their inherent power, and given it over to the hands of their enemy, the enemy of their soul. They are now **opposing themselves**, because they don't see the light; because they haven't repented; because they're not walking in the ways of God.

I'm not talking about those folks that aren't going to heaven. This instruction was given to true believers, but the devil's real weapon is deception. You've already been given by God all of the authority you need over the forces and the works of the devil. He's already under your feet. As far as God's concerned, it's already done. In Christ, we are already seated in heavenly places and the devil is under our feet.

But if you don't **know** that, then he'll be able to take your very authority and use it against you to attack you.

I've preached many times, "It's not what you know that's killing you; it's what you don't know that's killing you."

"My people are destroyed for lack of knowledge: because thou hast rejected knowledge, I will also reject thee, that thou shalt be no priest to me: seeing thou hast forgotten the law of thy God, I will also forget thy children."
—Hosea 4:6

Many are still being deceived. So it's not what you know that's killing you; it's what you don't know. Don't give yourself over or your stuff over to the enemy anymore. Don't let him take your authority and use it against you. Stop letting him take your words and use them against you. Stop letting him take your free will and use it against you. Stop opposing yourself. Stop allowing what belongs to you to be used against you.

DRUGS FUND TERRORISTS

I believe America's greatest sin is drug abuse, and this very sin has literally funded these terrorist groups. I don't know if you've seen this or not, but Afghanistan, where Osama bin Laden has been hiding for years, they have now grown to the point where they are the world's main source of opium. From opium comes heroin.

For years, Afghanistan has been growing this opium to be sold on U.S. streets, to our drug addicts on our streets. The U.S. dollars that it takes to buy those drugs to meet this horrible habit have found their way back and lined the pockets of Osama bin Laden and the terrorists that have now brought death to those same streets.

When I see our young boys and our girls hooked on these drugs, knowing that our money literally lined the pockets of our killers, I get mad. Our nation's own assets were used against us.

THE CHURCH UNDER END-TIME ATTACK

PARALLEL

THIS ATTACK WAS AN ATTACK ON FREEDOM AND LIBERTY ITSELF

Don't take my word for it. Take the word of our President. President George W. Bush said this: "Freedom itself was attacked this morning by a faceless coward. Freedom and fear are at war."

The initial name given to the U.S. mission to fight terrorism was "Operation Enduring Freedom." Why? This attack is not just an attack on America, or our people, or New York City, or Washington. It is an attack on freedom and liberty itself.

Make no mistake about this. Just as a hostile national enemy has desired to attack America's freedom and liberty, so too is our spiritual enemy afraid, intimidated and threatened by the freedom and the liberty within the Church of Jesus Christ.

Jesus said this in John, chapter 8: *"If the Son therefore shall make you free, you shall be free indeed."*

"Now the Lord is that Spirit: and where the Spirit of the Lord is, there is liberty."

—II Corinthians 3:17

Where the Spirit is in charge, there is liberty. Why? Because the Spirit of the Lord is the spirit of liberty. The Spirit of the Lord is the spirit of freedom.

Our freedom is intimidating to our enemy. He doesn't like it. He hates it. The spirit of Antichrist is loose on this earth. It wants to subvert freedom. It wants to control people. It wants to limit what they can do and not do. If you step out of line, it will cut off your head, or cut off your arm, or cut off your hand. Islam is a ruthless religion. Don't you let anybody try to lie and tell you it's a bunch of peacekeepers. No, it's ruthless.

When one studies the actual laws of Mohammed, one has to shed blood to get control over any nation that it has to this day. Look at their history books, where the law says, "You either preach Islam or your head comes off. If you even witness to somebody about Christ, we'll throw you in prison and maybe kill you." There's no freedom. There's no liberty there.

The enemy of your soul despises the spirit of liberty. Why is America great? Because of the freedoms and the liberties that are in this land. Where do you think those liberties and freedoms came from? They came out of the pages of the New Testament. They came out of the Spirit of the Lord that breathed upon this nation.

This battle between freedom and non-freedom is going to come to a head. Liberty and freedom can only come from the life flow of God's Spirit. That flow of life and that flow of the Spirit is what Satan himself is fearful of. President Bush's words were prophetic. They've been resonating in my spirit ever since I heard him say it. **Freedom and fear are at war**. That's the way it is in the spirit. In the spirit realm and the lives of every saint, there's a war.

In this hour you're going to be filled with one or the other. You're either going to be filled with the Spirit of the Lord and have freedom and liberty, or you're going to be filled with fear and the spirit of fear. There is a war between freedom and fear waging in your mind, in your life, in your home, and in your soul right now.

Notice the Apostle Paul's clear instructions to the saints in Galatia:

"Tell me, ye that desire to be under the law, do ye not hear the law? For it is written, that Abraham had two sons, the one by a bondmaid, the other by a freewoman. But he who was of the bondwoman was born after the flesh; but he of the freewoman was by promise."
—Galatians 4:21-23

Paul spells it out and shows the source once again of where this came from. Isn't it amazing that the Apostle Paul, in giving the Christian our thesis on liberty and freedom, in explaining it to us, goes right back to Abraham's two sons.

Now notice this clear line of demarcation that Paul spells out theologically. He says one is a bondwoman, meaning bondage, under control. And one is a free woman, meaning liberty and freedom.

You're going to be motivated by one or the other, the promise or the flesh. As a Christian, one of those two things is going to motivate you, the promise or the flesh. You choose which one controls you. You choose which one motivates you.

God is giving us a physical picture of what occurred, and then He's drawing spiritual parallels that apply to us spiritually. It's an allegory, or a prophetic picture.

"Which things are an allegory: for these are the two covenants; the one from the mount Sinai, which gendereth to bondage, which is Agar. For this Agar is mount Sinai in Arabia, and answereth to Jerusalem which now is, and is in bondage with her children. But Jerusalem which is above is free, which is the mother of us all. For it is written, Rejoice thou barren that bearest not; break forth and cry, thou that travailest not: for the desolate hath many more children than she which hath an husband. Now we, brethren, as Isaac was, are the children of promise. But as then he that was born after the flesh persecuted him that was born after the Spirit, even so it is now. Nevertheless what saith the scripture? Cast out the bondwoman and her son: for the son of the bondwoman shall not be heir with the son of the freewoman. So then, brethren, we are not children of the bondwoman, but of the free."
—Galatians 4:24-31

Paul is preaching to you what I have been preaching to you from the beginning of this book; and he is tying it to freedom. I don't know if I've ever seen anything more astounding to me in the Word of God. I'm telling you exactly what we are seeing transpire in our nation. Isn't this amazing?

Freedom is under attack in our nation. It was spelled out to us in the book of Galatians two thousand years ago that this would happen and this would come: that the son of the bondwoman, the son of Hagar, Ishmael and all his kids, would resent the promise, fight against the promise, and war against the promise. It's very, very clear.

He tells us to "Stand fast therefore in the liberty." What is this attack all about? It is an attack on liberty.

President Bush's words were prophetic: freedom and fear are at war in this hour. The Church is under end-time attack. And you're going to go one way or the other. This last day Church must walk in the true liberty and freedom of the Spirit.

Be on guard. Your enemy hates your liberty.

THE CHURCH UNDER END-TIME ATTACK

PARALLEL

7

AMERICA WAS ATTACKED BECAUSE OF HER SUPPORT OF ISRAEL

On the day of the attack, a film crew caught Palestinians in the West Bank handing out candy, honking their horns, waving their Palestinian flags, cheering and celebrating in the streets. The same day, a young Arab named Mostafa said this: *"I am in a dream. I never believed that one day the United States would come to pay a price for its support to Israel."*

From the Gaza, an Islamic Jihad official by the name of Nafez Assam said this: "What happened in the United States today is a consequence of American policies in this region."

How about Saddam Hussein's reference to international security. He made it very clear that the only way international security could be achieved for the United States was if the U.S.: "disengages itself from its evil alliance with Zionism."

If our supposed evil alliance with Zionism brings the wrath and the hatred of every Islamic leader and every Islamic terrorist, then let it be so. I will personally wear their hatred toward me as a badge of honor, because the very same God who gives me salvation today, and gives me forgiveness today, and gives me eternal life today, did so through a man who was born as a Hebrew man and was born in the womb of a young Jewish virgin.

If any enemy hates us, it ought to be because we did the right thing, the holy thing, the biblical thing, and stood with the nation of Israel.

The historical Church has by and large failed right here. If you study Church history, from the days of the Crusades to the great reformers and on, our history is littered with anti-Semitic hatred, where we too demonized the precious Jewish people. I'm telling you that when Hitler was able to lock them up, he did so with the support of ninety percent of the so-called evangelical Christian Church. Some of the same pamphlets that were used to bring about the Holocaust were littered with twisted verses and twisted statements of Christian leaders.

My God told me that the Jewish people were the apple of His eye. My God told me in His Word that He chose to give Abraham's seed that land. I will fight for her God-given right to live in and possess that land. I will fight for their right to live in that land with the same fervor I will fight for you and me to live in this land, because God could take this land away from us if He so chose. But He will never ever, ever, ever take that land in His mind and His heart away from His Covenant man, Abraham.

Genesis 12:3 makes it real clear: *"I will bless them that bless thee, and curse them that curseth thee."* Psalm 121:4 says, *"Behold, he that keepeth Israel shall neither slumber nor sleep."*

Previous generations of Christians have failed this important test. This last day Church must pass this test. We must stand with Israel.

"Replacement theology" is one of the greatest heresies that has ever been perpetrated on the Church of the Lord Jesus Christ, which says that somehow the Church has replaced Israel. No greater lie could ever be told. Romans 11 makes it very clear.

"I say then, Hath God cast away his people? God forbid. For I also am an Israelite, of the seed of Abraham, of the tribe of Benjamin. God hath not cast away his people which he foreknew. Wot ye not what the scripture saith of Elias? how he maketh intercession to God against Israel..."
—Romans 11:1-2

"I say then, Have they stumbled that they should fall? God forbid: but rather through their fall salvation is come unto the Gentiles, for to provoke them to jealousy....

"For if the casting away of them be the reconciling of the world, what shall the receiving of them be, but life from the dead?"
—Romans 11:11,15

The Old Testament prophets are filled with references where God will return His people to that very land and reestablish them. This says it's going to be like life from the dead. That's exactly what Israel is right now.

That's why the whole Islamic world can't stand Israel in that land today.

"For if thou wert cut out of the olive tree which is wild by nature, and wert grafted contrary to nature into a good olive tree: how much more shall these, which be the natural branches, be grafted into their own olive tree? For I would not, brethren, that ye should be ignorant of this mystery, lest ye should be wise in your own conceits; that blindness in part is happened to Israel, until the fulness of the Gentiles be come in. And so all Israel shall be saved: as it is written, There shall come out of Sion the Deliverer, and shall turn away ungodliness from Jacob: For this is my covenant unto them, when I shall take away their sins. As concerning the gospel, they are enemies for your sakes: but as touching the election, they are beloved for the fathers' sakes. For the gifts and calling of God are without repentance. For as ye in times past have not believed God, yet have now obtained mercy through their unbelief: Even so have these also now not believed, that through your mercy they also may obtain mercy."

—Romans 11:24-31

This should be our viewpoint. It's not that we don't want our precious Jewish brothers to come to the Lord, because they need to come to the Lord. One is not on their way to heaven just because they were born a Jew, absolutely not. You're a natural son of Abraham and God has a plan for your life. But now, you need to come to faith in your Messiah.

So we boldly preach that to any Jewish person that's listening. Our position must be that they are beloved for the Father's sake. We honor them, because without them we would not be. We are grafted into the vine.

We are to provoke the heart of the natural Jew to find the faith that their forefathers had. Of course we don't win them by calling them "Jesus killers." Never! They didn't kill Jesus. You and I killed Jesus. Your sin and my sin killed Jesus on the cross. Now he says just as their unbelief has caused you to find mercy, now you show mercy to them so that they through your mercy will find their faith.

America was attacked by the terrorists because we support and favor Israel, plain and simple.

THE CHURCH UNDER END-TIME ATTACK

OUR RESPONSE

After God showed me these seven spiritual parallels of how the attack on America parallels the Church being under attack, then He sat me down and He showed me seven responses.

He said, *"Son, observe how the nation responded. And the way that the nation responded to this attack I want the Church to learn from. Just as the attack revealed the schemes and the wiles of our enemy, so, too, America's response will speak warnings and instructions to the end time Church of how important it is we learn spiritual parallels from the specific responses by America's citizens."*

RESPONSE PARALLEL

OUR TRUE HEROES ARE ALWAYS THE COMMON, FACELESS, UNKNOWN FORCES OF THE FAITHFUL

As a result of this tragedy, one of the greatest responses of our nation has been we have finally recognized who our real, true heroes are. The Church must learn this lesson, because the Church for too long has done just what the world has done. We have elevated celebrities, and made celebrities our heroes, even in the Church, instead of our real, true strength.

Our real, true strength is people just like you. You love God. You're faithful to your spouse. You love your kids. You pay your bills. You pay your tithe. You come to church. You read your Bible. You pray. You are the faithful forces that make the Church strong.

In many cases, we have wrongly elevated the wrong people. We have taken our great preachers, and thank God for them; we have taken our great musicians, and thank God for them; but we've taken our Christian celebrities, our

Christian "stars," and we've said, "Well, they're our real strength."

They are not our real strength. It is the faithful forces of the faceless that are the strength of the Church.

Since 9-11, we have gotten back to the basics of elevating our true heroes. The Church, just like society and the world in recent years, has begun to elevate the wrong people. We've lifted up movie stars, and TV personalities, and musicians, and pro-athletes, and these are not the real true heroes. Real courage is not found within the ranks of the so-called stars, but rather it's found among those who are the servants among us.

Jesus said,

"But it shall not be so among you: but whosoever will be great among you, let him be your minister; And whosoever will be chief among you, let him be your servant: Even as the Son of man came not to be ministered unto, but to minister, and to give his life a ransom for many."
—Matthew 20:26-28

That is what God is looking for in this hour. He's not looking for spectacular giftings. He's looking for faithful servanthood, like someone who's willing to run into a building and give their life for someone else even if it means their life will be lost. That is what we are called to do in this hour in the Body of Christ, to lay down our life for others.

Don't think that once you preach a sermon, you'll be in the ministry. Don't think that when you write your first book, maybe you'll be in the ministry. No, when you serve in the nursery, you're in the ministry. When you serve and help our young children, you're in the ministry. When you help to usher or greet the people in church, you are in the ministry. The preacher is not the most important person in the church. The most important people in any church are the ushers and the greeters, and those who serve others. So don't look down, wherever you are at, look up!

Some people think, "Well, you know I don't preach good. I don't sing good. I don't get up in front of people." But maybe they are SERVING in the church on Sunday; that is the strength of the Church. That is the strength of the Body of Christ. It is our humble servants.

Jesus went on to say,

"But he that is greatest among you shall be your servant. And whosoever shall exalt himself shall be abased; and he that shall humble himself shall be exalted."
—Matthew 23:11-12

I'm reminded of the Apostle Paul. This great apostle and prophet, taken up to heaven many times, writer of two-thirds of the New Testament; do you know how he referred to himself?

Over and over again, if you read the Epistles that he wrote, at the very beginning, he would always refer to his servanthood first. He wrote, "I, Paul, a **servant** of Jesus Christ, called to be an apostle..." The first thing he said about himself was that he was just a simple servant, a "bondslave of Christ."

One of the Greek words for "servant" in the New Testament simply means "an under-rower." Picture a boat back in the time of the Roman Empire, two thousand years ago. The boats were run by manpower, men with strong arms and strong legs. You've seen those old movies, where they've got those guys down there underneath the boat, and they're all rowing. That's the picture being portrayed.

A servant is someone in the bottom of the boat faithfully rowing and rowing to reach a given destination.

You don't think of that as ministry, but God does. God says, *"If you want to be great in the Kingdom of God, be able to row this boat with your fellow believer."* You've got to work faithfully as a team. You've got to work as a team down there in that boat, to get somewhere.

Do you want to go somewhere in the Kingdom of God?

God says the way you do it is you don't just prophesy at the four winds every Sunday. Sometimes you just row and row, just stay at it. It isn't glamorous. Sometimes it isn't very much fun, but you just stay at it. You just stay serving. You just stay faithful.

"For though I be free from all men, yet have I made myself servant unto all, that I might gain the more."
—*I Corinthians 9:19*

Paul could have sat in the lap of luxury, but he chose not to.

I can't help but think of Acts, chapter 28, where Paul came upon a great storm. This great storm came in, wrecked the ship, and they found themselves out in the storm, literally deserted on an island. On this island, they're all wet and weary, with all the passengers and the crew stranded on this island.

Paul, instead of getting up and preaching a fire and brimstone message, the Bible says he went out and started picking up sticks for the fire. Paul gathered the sticks for the fire for all of the other wet, cold individuals on that boat. Out of it, a serpent came and latched onto him. He shook the serpent in the fire, and God redeemed him. He was not even harmed in any way.

Through that experience, every one was won to the Lord. Also, they took him to the leader of the island; God saved and healed that leader. Revival came to a whole nation and people group because one man became a servant. Instead of saying, "Well, I'm the big-time preacher here. Take care of me," he said, "No, I'm going to be a servant, and I'm going to make a fire to warm them."

You and I miss opportunities for ministry every day, because every opportunity for ministry is disguised as an opportunity to serve. If you will find an opportunity to serve, I promise you God will turn it into an opportunity to minister. After September 11th, people's hearts became open to the Gospel.

Be a servant, ready to serve. We must repent from our "celebrity spirit mentality." Christian, stop thinking of yourself as unimportant merely because you seemingly go unnoticed in your service to God.

The Church's greatest strength has always been her faithful servants. We must relearn this in this end time hour. I've said for years now, this final move of God, **it will not be the big *"some-body,"* but rather it will be *His body*.**

This end time move of God is not going to be the big stardom. It's going to be the faithful forces of the Body of Christ.

Thank God for the great men. They need to keep doing what they're doing. But the same anointing, the same miracles, the same harvest, and the same God that moves with our well-known ministers is going to move through your hands, your lips, and your life right where you're at.

Don't limit how God's going to use you! Be ready for the harvest. Be ready for miracles. You've got hands. You've got faith. You've got a tongue. Use it in the Name of the Lord. It's the time for the Body of Christ to be the Body of Christ. So observe and learn! Just as America is now seeing, the real true heroes within the Church are her common, faceless, unknown faithful servants.

THE CHURCH UNDER END-TIME ATTACK

RESPONSE PARALLEL

$$\boxed{\mathbf{2}}$$

OUR GREATEST RESOLVE IS BORN IN THE MIDST OF OUR GREATEST PAIN

September 11, 2001, has already been called another "Pearl Harbor." After the 1941 Pearl Harbor attack, Japan's leader made a now infamous statement when he said, "I fear that all we have done is awaken a sleeping giant." America reached greatness as a result of the resolve after Pearl Harbor. Don't make any mistake about it. Other nations were primary nations around this globe, but after Pearl Harbor, America got involved and put down the enemy of Nazism, and put down an evil regime.

Out of the ashes of the loss of those lives came a greater resolve, and the greatness was born out of great pain. Now the Church must learn this lesson.

I'm reminded of what Dr. Billy Graham said after the terrorist attacks: "What our enemy intended to destroy us has backfired and backlashed."

Not all obstacles are bad. We've got to relearn this. In fact, an opportunity's favorite disguise is usually as an obstacle. Conflict is simply meeting an obstacle on the road to your answer. America is on the road for revival because the saints have been praying. September 11th is a great opportunity that God has given this nation to find revival.

The Apostle Paul put it best when he said, "We are pressed on every side by troubles, but we're not crushed or broken." He said, "We're perplexed, and we don't know why these things happen as they do. But we don't give up and quit." Paul said, "We are hunted down, but God never abandons us. We get knocked down, but we get back up and keep fighting" (II Corinthians 4:8-9).

That's the attitude of the winner. That's the attitude that the Church needs in this hour. We've got to learn this lesson. Our greatest resolve should be born out of this pain. Being a Christian doesn't remove you from the world and its problems. Some are preaching, "Just get enough anointing. Just get enough Word. Just get enough faith. You'll never have any tests."

That is absolutely false. The closer I get to God, the more the enemy comes to test and challenge my faith.

They left Paul for dead many times. They whipped him and stoned him. The devil did everything he could to stop that man. Why? Because he got close to God. Christianity never does teach you that you're going to be removed from the world and its problems. Rather, we teach that it's going to equip you to live in it victoriously!

No one is immune to problems. Even the lion has to fight off the flies. Church, we're the lion. Instead of the Church being afraid of the devil, the devil ought to be afraid of the Church! Christians should not run from bad times, evil times, and from demon spirits. We ought to have every demon in town running from us. Chase them down.

Do you see how you can turn it around?

Don't be like the masses of the Hebrew army quaking under the sound of Goliath's voice, in their holy huddle, wringing their hands in fear. Take on a spirit of a warrior. Have some resolve about you like David did. He said, "Hey, I slew a bear; and I slew a lion. Who is this uncircumcised Philistine? You need to repent and come to the God of the Covenant; or you're about to lose your head." That's what we should do with trouble. That's what we ought to do with problems. That's what we should do with obstacles.

Turn it around!

Growth and success don't eliminate obstacles, they merely create new ones. Be glad you're doing something good. Be glad you're doing something right. God is working on us and walking with us. Be glad you are worthy of the devil's attention.

One man once said, "The block of granite, which was an obstacle in the pathway of the weak, becomes a stepping stone in the pathway of the strong." Obstacles are part of life.

Jesus said,

"These things I have spoken unto you, that in me ye might have peace. In the world ye shall have tribulation: but be of good cheer; I have overcome the world."
—*John 16:33*

Jesus did not say, "There's no storm." He said, "No, I am here in the midst of the storm."

The difference between iron and steel is fire. The fire tried the steel and proved it. It made it worthy. God never promised that it would be easy. But He said this: "Trust me. Believe in me, for all things are possible to he that believes." In the presence of trouble, some people grow wings, and others buy crutches.

Which one are you?

When God is at your side, He helps you face the music, even when you don't like the tune. Sometimes I've got to wake up and "face the music." I didn't write that song, but I'm going to play it anyhow.

Don't just look to God through your circumstances. Look at your circumstances through God.

Your problem is your promotion. We look at September 11th as this terrible tragedy; and of course it is, rightfully so. No one's denying that. But this is where the waters are about to part. This is where we're going to find our resolve as a nation. We, as the Church of Jesus Christ, have got to learn this lesson. Your problem isn't your problem. Your problem is your promotion.

A whole army of Hebrew soldiers saw Goliath as a problem, and they quaked in fear. One man, little David, saw Goliath as a promotion, and with a little stone, took him down.

The door of opportunity always swings on little hinges of opposition. And I've learned something about progress: Problems are the price of progress. The obstacles of life are intended to make us better, not bitter.

Obstacles are merely a call to strengthen, not to quit. Don't lose your resolve. A great man I know says this: "Between you and anything significant will be giants in your path." Lou Holtz, the great football coach, said, "Adversity is another way to measure the greatness of individuals. I never had a crisis that didn't make me stronger."

Hear those words, because they're biblical, they're spiritual. I believe they're accurate. I never had a crisis that didn't make me stronger.

This tragedy has knocked us to our knees, but that's precisely where God wanted us to be all along. On our knees, we will pray. On our knees we will repent. On our knees, we will return to God. We stand tallest when we're on our knees. The strongest action that a person can take in any situation is to go to their knees and ask God for help. Don't miss this, Christian: **Great resolve is born in the midst of great pain.**

THE CHURCH UNDER END-TIME ATTACK

RESPONSE PARALLEL

UNITY

What the enemy tried to do to separate us has brought this nation together in ways more profound than anything ever could have done. This nation, regardless of whether they're Republican or Democrat, they're singing on the steps of the Capitol Building. There is now a newfound unity. This nation is united as a people unlike anything I have ever seen in my life.

From a historical standpoint, since Pearl Harbor there has never been a single event that has so united this nation as this tragedy has. Now you'd think in good times we'd have enough sense to get together. But the reality is that it's usually tough times, hard times, and times of crisis and difficulty, we get together. It's like God has a way of saying, "Well, if you're not going to get together by yourselves, then I'll just push you together."

You thought it was the devil, but it was God pushing you together, even with strangers. It was God bringing us together. Democrat and Republican, Jew and Christian, all of us were praying together? That's God!

Bishop T. D. Jakes said, "Somewhere in the Red, White and Blue, is you." We may have come over here on different boats, but we're in the same boat now. We're all together now. There's great strength in unity. There's a power that comes to God's people when we are united. As long as we allow things, whatever they are, to separate us, we are not as effective as we need to be, and as effective as we should be, and as effective as we could be for God.

"Now I beseech you, brethren, by the name of our Lord Jesus Christ, that ye all speak the same thing, and that there be no divisions among you; but that ye be perfectly joined together in the same mind and in the same judgment."
—I Corinthians 1:10

You need to understand this: Satan himself fears a truly united Church. When the Church is united, hell trembles.

This is Jesus' High Priestly prayer:

"Neither pray I for these alone, but for them also which shall believe on me through their word; That they all may be one; as thou, Father, art in me, and I in thee, that they also may be one in us: that the world may believe that thou hast sent me."
—John 17:20-21

Verse 21 gives us the prayer of Jesus: "That they all may be one!" Now here's why: "that the world may believe."

We've come up with all kinds of evangelism strategies. Thank God for every one of them, because people need to get saved. But I'm going to tell you something: We've neglected the greatest evangelistic strategy that our Lord Himself gave us. He said, "When a lost world finally sees my people as one, then they'll believe that you sent me."

I hear a crying, lost world saying, "Why do I need your Jesus? Why do I need your Christianity, when you guys can't even get along? You fight over those words you use when you baptize. The Church fights over the way you take communion. You fight over whether the carpet's blue or red. Then you fight over music - whether it's long, slow or fast. You fight over all these dumb things. The Church can't even get together. You think I need your Jesus?"

Unfortunately, that's what the world says.

The world is watching us, as Christians. They are looking for a united people to say, "Look, we may differ on other things behind closed doors, but as far as you're concerned, we are a united front."

That's what our government is doing right now. They may disagree behind closed doors, but they're a united front when they come out in public, during times of war. There are many things that we've thrown out before the world to observe, our in-house bickering that should have remained behind closed doors. And the world scoffs at us. The world makes fun of us.

The world makes fun of our Christianity and our faith, because we've not done what Jesus said.

Now keep reading, because here comes the best part.

"And the glory which thou gavest me I have given them; that they may be one, even as we are one: I in them, and thou in me, that they may be made perfect in one; and that the world may know that thou hast sent me, and hast loved them, as thou hast loved me."

—John 17:22-23

I submit to you that the glory that is reserved for the final generation will come to a Church that is one. We are that glorious Church without spot or wrinkle that's going to be "caught up" at His appearing.

Do you believe Jesus is coming soon?

He's got to do something to bring us together as ONE.

Many preachers are preaching this message now. But in January, 2001, I taught,

"There are many evidences that America, as well as the rest of the world, is about to enter a powerful season of revival just as Israel did at Mizpeh. First and foremost, historical walls of racial separation in the Church are dissolving, and unity, based upon repentance, is becoming a reality.

"Racial and denominational barriers are melting. Christians from a variety of different streams of doctrine and emphasis are hugging and loving each other in a variety of non-denominational movements. The greatest threat to Satan's domain is the unity of the Church. The Church will be perfected when she comes into unity. When she does, the whole world will understand that Jesus certainly was sent by the Father. This will go beyond completing the Great Commission. True unity will not come from any person or movement seeking to bring on unity. It will not come through ecumenical movements, political compromises, or the attempt by men to bring about unity, regardless of how noble they may seem. As the Father answers the prayer of His Son, the living Church will discover the blessings and power coming together.

"The outcome will be a vast multitude in the world will believe, and on an unequalled scale, revival will come to the earth."

What a truly prophetic word.

None of us could have foreseen what transpired on September 11th, with its terrible ramifications. But I've got news for you. God's an economical God. God didn't cause this tragedy, but He's going to use it as a wake-up call to this nation and to His Church! We've got to unite. Just like our nation is coming together, the Church of Jesus Christ is coming together.

You're strong without me. I'm strong without you. But neither you nor I are as strong as when we're united. The Bible seems to indicate ten times and tenfold stronger, when we are together.

"How should one chase a thousand, and two put ten thousand to flight, except their Rock had sold them, and the LORD had shut them up?"

—Deuteronomy 32:30

So it is time that we let the Church major on the majors and not on the minors, because we've got to get together. We've got to walk together.

We are like a family. I doubt everything always runs just perfectly without any kind of conflict or disharmony twenty-four hours a day, every day of the week, every week of the month, every month of the year in your house; because if there's more than one person in that house, there's an "opportunity for negotiation," let's just say.

We have to negotiate when we live together. If we're in the same house, there's going to be some compromise. There's going to be some rough edges on me that you see, and rough edges on you that I see. Somewhere along the line, I've got to love you enough to work with you, because I value you; because when we're family, I can't turn my back on you. I can't leave you. I'm with you. You're with me. We're stuck together. So learn to walk together. Learn to walk with one another.

Don't let some little petty thing offend you to the point that you flee and run. Where God's planted you in a family, you stay. Don't you be offended in your church simply because the sermon went too long, or the air wasn't too cold, or the song was too loud, or somebody came and is sitting in your seat on Sunday morning, or some other circumstance. We've got to work together!

Why?

It isn't about you and me. It's about them. It's about the harvest. It's about all those that the Lord wants to reach in this hour.

"Behold, how good and how pleasant it is for brethren to dwell together in unity!
"It is like the precious ointment upon the head, that ran down upon the beard, even Aaron's beard: that went down to the skirts of his garments;
"As the dew of Hermon, and as the dew that descended upon the mountains of Zion: for there the LORD commanded the blessing, even life for evermore."
—Psalm 133:1-3

You see, I don't know about you, but I don't want to go anywhere without His blessing. So that means that I am going to do whatever it takes to keep His blessing. I'm going to do whatever it takes to keep that anointing, that presence of God, and that blessing of God on my life. That means I'm going to dwell together in unity. I'm not going to just dwell with my brethren.

It's not just dwell together and just kind of tolerate each other. No. There's a difference between just putting up with one another and just kind of tolerating one another, and real unity.

Real unity is when I value you. Real unity is when I cherish you. Real unity is when I esteem you. Real unity is when I lift you up above myself, and I say, "There is a valuable part

of my family." "When I esteem my brethren above myself."
God says, "**There** at that place of unity, I will command my
blessing." We must believe that and act accordingly, especially
in these end-time days!

THE CHURCH UNDER END-TIME ATTACK

RESPONSE PARALLEL

OUR IN-HOUSE NEGLIGENCE AND LETHARGY IMMEDIATELY CHANGED

We, as a nation, were lulled into thinking that we were safe. But we weren't, were we? It was a false safety. It was a false security. It was a false hope. We thought that surely a terrorist act of this proportion could never come to our shores. However, we were mistaken. We were wrong. We weren't safe.

So what happened?

Our nation's spirit had to change. The climate of our nation is now different since September 11th. We were lethargic and negligent previously, but now we're on the watch. Now we're on guard. That lethargy had to be turned around.

It is the exact same way with the Church.

Our spiritual lethargy is lethal. Just as America has now awakened at this hour, the Church is now awake at this hour. This is a wakeup call! Man of God after man of God has been saying the same thing. Anybody that's got any discernment can tell that this tragedy was a wakeup call for our nation. That's what I'm trying to say.

We had to be shaken from our in-house negligence, lethargy and lukewarmness. It's a Laodicean climate. This is nothing new to scriptures. In fact God declared that the end time Church would have to deal with the spirit of Laodicea, this lukewarmness, neither hot nor cold.

If there's ever been a spirit in recent days that has infiltrated the Church in America, it's the Laodicean spirit, the lukewarm spirit. So God had to wake us up.

Suddenly prayer is allowed in our schools. Suddenly everyone is now calling on God and singing "God Bless America."

The Holy Spirit spoke to me and said, "Turn 'God Bless America' around to 'America, Bless God'!" It's time that we don't just say, "God, bless us"; rather say, "God, how can we bless you? How can we be a part of what you're doing? We want to bless your name."

The Bible says, "If God be for us, who can be against us?" But do you know what that presupposes? That presupposes that you and I are on the right side. That presupposes that we're **with** Him. "If God be for you, who can be against you?" That means you'd better be on His side.

The Bible says that judgment begins in the House of God. We want God to "Judge those sinners. Oh God, judge those terrible people. Oh God, judge those terrorists."

But God is saying, "No. Before I get to dealing with them, I've got some things to deal with you. I want to deal with your lukewarm spirit first!" So you'd better be on His side.

"And unto the angel of the church of the Laodiceans write; These things saith the Amen, the faithful and true witness, the beginning of the creation of God; I know thy works, that thou art neither cold nor hot: I would thou wert cold or hot. So then **because thou art lukewarm,** *and neither cold nor hot, I will spue thee out of my mouth. Because thou sayest, I am rich, and increased with goods, and have need of nothing; and knowest not that thou art wretched, and miserable, and poor, and blind, and naked: I counsel thee to buy of me gold tried in the fire, that thou mayest be rich; and white raiment, that thou mayest be clothed, and that the shame of thy nakedness do not appear; and anoint thine eyes with eyesalve, that thou mayest see. As many as I love, I rebuke and chasten: be zealous therefore, and repent. Behold, I stand at the door, and knock: if any man hear my voice, and open the door, I will come in to him, and will sup with him, and he with me."*
—Revelation 3:14-20

This scripture refers to the last Church. All scholars believe that these seven churches of Asia Minor, the seven churches of Revelation, are chronological. The last one will be the Laodicean Church, previous to the Lord's Coming.

Jesus is talking to His people, the Church—not sinners! This is His end time Church He's talking to, you and me.

Doesn't that sound like He is talking about the majority of American Christianity? We're rich, increased with goods, in need of nothing.

When Jesus says "REPENT" in the above scripture, He is not talking to the world...it is the Christians. We want the heathens to repent. We want the sinners to repent. We want the drug-pushers to repent. We want the pornographers to repent. We want the politicians to repent.

God says, "I want *you* to repent."

"If my people, which are called by my name, shall humble themselves, and pray, and seek my face, and turn from their wicked ways; then will I hear from heaven, and will forgive their sin, and will heal their land."
—II Chronicles 7:14

We want the heathen to turn from their wicked ways. God's going to deal with them. But He's going to deal with you first.

"Behold, I stand at the door, and knock: if any man hear my voice, and open the door, I will come in to him, and will sup with him, and he with me.
"To him that overcometh will I grant to sit with me in my throne."
—Revelation 3:20-21

We read those scriptures and say, "Oh yeah, He's knocking on the door of the sinner's heart." Well, that's true. But you're pulling it completely out of context to use it in that way because He's not talking to sinners here. He's not talking to the unbelievers. He's talking to His people, His Church. In other words, Jesus is knocking on the door of the heart of the last day Church, saying, *"Let me in. Let me in. Let me come in. Sup with me. And me sup with you."* We have a religious fervor in many churches, but too often we do not want to get so close that we sup with Him, or have intimacy with Him. God talks about the Church in the last days as *"perilous times...having a form of godliness, but denying the power thereof " (II Timothy 3:1,5).*

Jesus said, *"There are going to be those that will come to me and say, 'Oh, we did this in your name, and we did that in your name, and we prophesied in your name, and we built great churches in your name, and we just did all these great things in your name' " (Matthew 7:22-23).* And He will say, *"Depart from me, I never knew you."*

And the word there is a word for "know" that means "intimacy; intimate knowledge." It's not that they weren't saved, and weren't even in heaven, and weren't in the presence of God. But He said, "I never knew you intimately."

God is saying to the Church this very day, "Watch the response of your nation. They've awakened out of sleep. They've awakened out of lethargy. Now, Church, you do the same thing!"

Leonard Ravenhill, the great revivalist, said, *"The only reason America does not have revival is because we are content to live without it.*" That is oh so powerful and so true. I pray that after September 11th that's no longer the case.

I believe that if we'll be content without revival, we'll never see it. We've got to get hungry again. We've got to get thirsty again. We've got to get desperate again. I don't want to be content. I'm going to stay un-content, spiritually. "Content" means "self-satisfied." God, remove from us this spiritual contentment, and cause us to be hungry and thirsty again.

THE CHURCH UNDER END-TIME ATTACK

RESPONSE PARALLEL

THE STOCK MARKET PLUMMETED

Our stock market plummeted. No one wants our economy to fail. I hope we see full recovery of our economy. I really do. I'm not pronouncing a woe or lack of recovery for our economy in what you're about to read, but this is a fact which must be seen.

Are you aware that the greatest single drop in American history occurred the day that they reopened the stock market in the New York Stock Exchange? It outdid the Great Depression. I am told that the market lost one trillion dollars of value in one day. One day, a trillion dollars! Think of it.

Now, why is that important? Did you know that Jesus had more to say about money than He did heaven or hell combined? The Bible centers on it a whole lot, probably more than you think or more than you realize.

"Lay not up for yourselves treasures upon earth, where moth and rust doth corrupt, and where thieves break through and steal: But lay up for yourselves treasures in heaven, where neither moth nor rust doth corrupt, and where thieves do not break through nor steal: For where your treasure is, there will your heart be also."

—Matthew 6:19-21

Could it be that our trust has been in the wrong place? Isn't that at least possible? Is it possible that we have trusted our economic might instead of the God who gave it to us? Is it possible that we got our eyes off of treasures in heaven and put them on treasures on this earth? Is it possible that before God is going to come with a sweeping move of revival across our land, He's going to touch the idol of our hearts? I think it's possible.

"Go to now, ye rich men, weep and howl for your miseries that shall come upon you. Your riches are corrupted, and your garments are motheaten. Your gold and silver is cankered; and the rust of them shall be a witness against you, and shall eat your flesh as it were fire. Ye have heaped treasure together for the last days."

—James 5:1-3

God is saying here prophetically that there is going to be something that occurs to the wealth of those who have heaped up treasure in the last days. Thank God He's not through, because He goes down in verses 7 and 8, saying, "Be patient therefore, brethren, unto the coming of the Lord. Behold, the husbandman waiteth for the precious fruit of the earth, and hath long patience for it, until he receive the early and latter rain."

God dealt with me strongly from those verses and showed me that's why Jesus hasn't come back to the earth.

God is saying, "Look, you need to have your eyes on the great harvest of the earth."

If we are not using whatever wealth and prosperity that God has given us for the sake of winning the harvest of the earth, then we've missed the whole thing. If all we're doing is building bigger houses, bigger barns, and nicer clothes and bigger cars, then we've missed the whole point. I believe it's time that we deal with this area of our life. God has *a harvest of souls* on His mind for this final hour.

There are two systems at work in this final hour. There's the world system and the world's system of economy. And then there's God's system. There's an earthly economy and there's a heavenly economy. Banks can fail, stocks can fall and companies can collapse. But God can provide and bless even in the midst of bad economic happenings for the sake of the harvest. Our Lord is the Lord of the harvest!

Let me remind you Philippians 4:19 is still true. It says, *"But my God shall supply all my need according to His riches in glory by Christ Jesus."* I believe there's a place in God, when your priorities are right and your trust and your confidence is in the right place, where God's provision will come forth supernaturally. I believe it.

God is challenging the Church in this hour to trust Him with their money. Stop trusting in earthly investments and uncertain riches, and step into faith. And see God bring in supernatural provision to meet your every need, while you become a channel to assist in the great end time harvest.

Deuteronomy 8:18 is still true: ***"But thou shalt remember the Lord thy God: for it is He that gives you power to get wealth."*** Now, why? "So that He might establish His covenant" in the earth. God's not opposed to His people having wealth. God needs His people to have wealth.

But God is also saying, "Look, your priorities have got to come in line. If you're trusting in your stuff, I'm going to mess with your stuff. Your trust better be in me."

God wants to give provision and harvest to us. It is going to come supernaturally. God can perform supernatural financial miracles, only if your heart is in the right place.

God wants your heart. He said, "Where your treasure is, there will your heart be also." I want my treasure to be in souls. I want my treasures to be in heavenly bank accounts. I don't want my treasures down here.

That doesn't mean I don't want to pay my bills, because I do want to pay my bills. I want you to pay your bills, too. And if you don't live in a nice enough house and you deserve a better one, God can give you a better one. But our priority must be to use our finances to reach a lost world.

That's why you're a threat to the enemy with your finances, because he knows what you'll do with it. That's why he fights it like he does with you and me, because he knows, anything we get will go back into God's Kingdom!

This is the hour of ingathering, and our hearts, our attention and our focus must be on the harvest.

THE CHURCH UNDER END-TIME ATTACK

RESPONSE PARALLEL

THIS NEW WAR WILL BE A LONG HAUL, NOT A SHORT STRUGGLE

Now observe that and learn. This new war will be a long haul, not a short struggle. Starting with our President and following down with all the military generals and leaders, they've all told us that this war on terrorism has only begun. "There may be many years involved in this war."

Unlike the Gulf War of 1991, which was only less than one hundred days of battle, this war will be a protracted war. There will be a protracted struggle.

Now, what's the point? The point is this: Our war with our spiritual enemy is a lifetime struggle.

Spiritually, like we've already read in Ephesians 6, when you've done all to stand, you stand, and you continue to stand. If you're standing today, you've got to stand tomorrow. If you stand tomorrow, you've got to stand the next day. There's no sitting down in this battle.

John 10:10 says, *"The thief comes to steal, kill and destroy: But I am come that you might have life, and have it more abundantly."* If His abundance is promised for your lifetime, and that means the last part of that verse is for your lifetime, then I submit that the first part is for your lifetime too. The thief is going to come to steal, kill and destroy, today, and tomorrow, and next week.

Your Christian struggle, your Christian life isn't a quick sprint. It's a marathon. The Apostle Paul, in his writings, likens the Christian faith unto a race. In fact at the end of his life, Paul made it very clear; he said,

"I have fought a good fight, I have finished my course, I have kept the faith: Henceforth there is laid up for me a crown of righteousness, which the Lord, the righteous judge, shall give me at that day: and not to me only, but unto all them also that love his appearing."
—II Timothy 4:7-8

If you love His appearing, there is a crown for you. I'm praying, "Lord Jesus, even so, come quickly, Lord Jesus." If I'm looking for His appearing, the Bible says there's a special crown awaiting us that Paul received. But he had to run his race.

Over the years, I've seen people start out real good, only to finish real bad. We're real good at starting stuff and not so good at finishing. I want to finish this race. I don't want to just run, and then lose it at the end. You're not in a quick sprint. You're in a marathon.

That's the difference between these wars. The response here is very clear. We're in it for the long haul.

We've already read the verse in II Timothy, chapter 2: "Endure hardness, as a good soldier of Jesus Christ." We are soldiers. Soldiers can't take vacations, and soldiers can't go AWOL. They can, but they get in trouble.

A lot of Christians are AWOL. Do you know what "AWOL" means? It means "absent without leave." Don't be absent without leave. Be on the job. Be on duty.

The great Reformer, Martin Luther, said, *"If I profess with the loudest voice and clearest exposition every portion of the Truth of God except precisely that little point, which the world and the devil are at that moment attacking, I'm not confessing Christ, however boldly I may be professing Christ. For where the battle rages, there the loyalty of the soldier is proved. And to be steady on all the battlefield besides is mere flight and disgrace if he flinches at that point."*

That's profound. That's powerful. He's saying that the battle is not going to end with just one bombing, or with one day's victory, or one Sunday mountaintop experience. He's saying, "Be prepared for the long haul."

THE CHURCH UNDER END-TIME ATTACK

RESPONSE PARALLEL

7

NATIONWIDE, U.S. CITIZENS BEGAN TO GIVE THEIR BLOOD AND THEIR MONEY

Do you know that the Red Cross received record-high amounts of finances and blood since September 11th? You probably saw like I did, the lines of people all over the nation after September 11th. They said, "I don't know what I can do, but I'm going to do something. I'm going to do my part." They got in line for several hours. Why? To give their blood.

America gave more blood than ever before, in record numbers, and donations to relief agencies reached all-time high record figures. There were celebrities and musicians; and there was a TV special and many more that followed, and they literally raised hundreds of millions of dollars.

And the Church, too, must rise to the task and the challenge and give our blood and give our funds. Your blood represents your life.

The president of the Red Cross resigned and stepped down because there has been so much money that the Red Cross has received in the last few weeks that there were in-house fights over how to spend that money. Behind closed doors, the leaders and officials of the Red Cross literally were fighting amongst themselves about what to do with the hundreds of millions of dollars that were received. It's almost like America gave too much money.

My immediate reaction was, "That's an indictment against the Church," because most ministries suffered horrendous income losses the three months after September 11th.

There's something here the Church has got to learn. I believe God wants the Church in such a fashion where we've got to have in-house disputes over what we're going to do with all the money that's inside our doors. God's done that before, do you know that? You study your history of the Old Testament, and there came a day where the King said, "Don't bring anymore."

I want to be faithful with what God's given me. Do you know what the Apostle Paul taught in I Corinthians, chapter 6? He said, *"Your body is the temple of the Holy Ghost. You are not your own. For you are bought with a price: therefore glorify God in your body, and in your spirit, which are God's."*

If you are a child of God you are not your own. It's time we recognized that we've got to stop living for ourselves. America gave their blood and gave their money. It is time for the Church to give their blood, their life, and their money. Jesus said, *"If you try to hold onto your life, you are going to lose it; but, if you lose it for my sake then you will find it."*

Do you believe God wants you to overcome? First John 4:4 says, *"Greater is He that's in me than he that's in the world."* We can overcome this end time attack, this assault and be victorious. Do you believe it? Do you know how we're going to do it?

"And they overcame him by the blood of the Lamb, and by the word of their testimony; and they loved not their lives unto the death."

—Revelation 12:11

Do you know what the word "witness" means in the Greek language, when it says in Acts 1:8, *"But ye shall receive power, after that the Holy Ghost is come upon you: and ye shall be witnesses unto me both in Jerusalem, and in all Judaea, and in Samaria, and unto the uttermost part of the earth"?*

It's the same Greek word translated "martyr." This is an hour when we'd better give our blood, our life and our finances.

You understand that you and I live in a moment that we've not lived in before, that no one has lived in before. This is the very end of days and the end of time. Jesus is going to wrap this thing up and return soon.

Do you understand that God has promised the earth that in the latter days the glory on the latter house would be greater than the glory on the former house? God has promised in

His Word that in the very end of days, He was going to pour out of His Spirit like rain and the last day Church was going to receive the early and the latter rain.

God has promised the earth that there would be an army in the last days. He said, "I'm going to come back for a glorious Church without spot or wrinkle." My friend, we're it. It's you and it's me.

America is suddenly serious about things she's never been serious before about. I believe it's time for the Church to be strong!

God has waited for this hour, this final hour, where He will have a people and a body in the earth who will lose their lives, and who will pay the price necessary to yield themselves to His Holy Spirit and allow God's life to be lived through them. God said, *"That will be an overcoming Church."*

The Church is under a unique end time attack, but we can overcome. You can overcome.

Be ready...for Jesus is coming soon!

For further information, please contact:

Dr. Joe Van Koevering
God's News Behind the News
P.O. Box 10475
St. Petersburg, FL 33733
www.godsnews.org